MW01505889

Thanks for buying our book!

For a free
printable, email

paperpeonypress@gmail.com

and we will send
something fun to
your inbox!

for the love of books

PAPER PEONY PRESS

PAPER PEONY

book club

We love seeing all the books you're reading
and how you're keeping track of all those
great reads! Post on social media with hastag
#paperpeonybookclub
and can join our growing community of book lovers!

For the Love of Books: A Reading Journal for Teens
© Paper Peony Press.
First Edition, 2023

Published by: Paper Peony Press
@paperpeonypress
www.paperpeonypress.com

For wholesale inquiries contact: reagan@paperpeonypress.com

Printed in China

978-1952842986

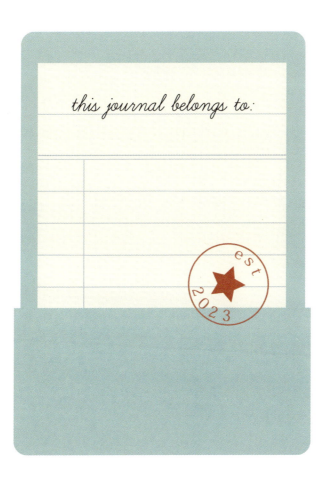

this journal belongs to:

est 2023

TABLE OF
Contents

Daily Reading Tracker

	Jan.	Feb.	March	April	May	June	July	Aug.	Sept.	Oct.	Nov.	Dec.
1	■	■	■	■	■	■	■	■	■	■	■	■
2	■	■	■	■	■	■	■	■	■	■	■	■
3	■	■	■	■	■	■	■	■	■	■	■	■
4	■	■	■	■	■	■	■	■	■	■	■	■
5	■	■	■	■	■	■	■	■	■	■	■	■
6	■	■	■	■	■	■	■	■	■	■	■	■
7	■	■	■	■	■	■	■	■	■	■	■	■
8	■	■	■	■	■	■	■	■	■	■	■	■
9	■	■	■	■	■	■	■	■	■	■	■	■
10	■	■	■	■	■	■	■	■	■	■	■	■
11	■	■	■	■	■	■	■	■	■	■	■	■
12	■	■	■	■	■	■	■	■	■	■	■	■
13	■	■	■	■	■	■	■	■	■	■	■	■
14	■	■	■	■	■	■	■	■	■	■	■	■
15	■	■	■	■	■	■	■	■	■	■	■	■
16	■	■	■	■	■	■	■	■	■	■	■	■
17	■	■	■	■	■	■	■	■	■	■	■	■
18	■	■	■	■	■	■	■	■	■	■	■	■
19	■	■	■	■	■	■	■	■	■	■	■	■
20	■	■	■	■	■	■	■	■	■	■	■	■
21	■	■	■	■	■	■	■	■	■	■	■	■
22	■	■	■	■	■	■	■	■	■	■	■	■
23	■	■	■	■	■	■	■	■	■	■	■	■
24	■	■	■	■	■	■	■	■	■	■	■	■
25	■	■	■	■	■	■	■	■	■	■	■	■
26	■	■	■	■	■	■	■	■	■	■	■	■
27	■	■	■	■	■	■	■	■	■	■	■	■
28	■	■	■	■	■	■	■	■	■	■	■	■
29	■	■	■	■	■	■	■	■	■	■	■	■
30	■		■	■	■	■	■	■	■	■	■	■
31	■		■		■		■	■		■		■

TITLE / AUTHOR:

WANT IT HAVE IT READ!

○ ○ ○
○ ○ ○
○ ○ ○
○ ○ ○
○ ○ ○
○ ○ ○
○ ○ ○
○ ○ ○
○ ○ ○
○ ○ ○
○ ○ ○
○ ○ ○
○ ○ ○
○ ○ ○
○ ○ ○
○ ○ ○
○ ○ ○
○ ○ ○
○ ○ ○
○ ○ ○
○ ○ ○
○ ○ ○

Use these pages to keep a list of all the books you
want to read. Make your way through the checklist
for each title as you go!

TITLE / AUTHOR:

WANT IT   HAVE IT   READ!

Literary Bucket List

TITLE / AUTHOR:

_____ ○ ○ ○
_____ ○ ○ ○
_____ ○ ○ ○
_____ ○ ○ ○
_____ ○ ○ ○
_____ ○ ○ ○
_____ ○ ○ ○
_____ ○ ○ ○
_____ ○ ○ ○
_____ ○ ○ ○
_____ ○ ○ ○
_____ ○ ○ ○
_____ ○ ○ ○
_____ ○ ○ ○
_____ ○ ○ ○
_____ ○ ○ ○
_____ ○ ○ ○
_____ ○ ○ ○
_____ ○ ○ ○
_____ ○ ○ ○
_____ ○ ○ ○
_____ ○ ○ ○
_____ ○ ○ ○
_____ ○ ○ ○
_____ ○ ○ ○

Literary Bucket List

TITLE / AUTHOR:

HISTORICAL FICTION

TITLE	RATING
AUTHOR	★ ★ ★ ★ ★

SCIENCE FICTION

TITLE	RATING
AUTHOR	★ ★ ★ ★ ★

BIOGRAPHY

TITLE	RATING
AUTHOR	★ ★ ★ ★ ★

CLASSIC LITERATURE

TITLE	RATING
AUTHOR	★ ★ ★ ★ ★

MYSTERY

TITLE	RATING
AUTHOR	★ ★ ★ ★ ★

THRILLER

TITLE	RATING
AUTHOR	★ ★ ★ ★ ★

ROMANCE

TITLE	RATING
AUTHOR	★ ★ ★ ★ ★

PERSONAL DEVELOPMENT

TITLE	RATING
AUTHOR	⭐ ⭐ ⭐ ⭐ ⭐

MEMOIR

TITLE	RATING
AUTHOR	⭐ ⭐ ⭐ ⭐ ⭐

BIOGRAPHY

TITLE	RATING
AUTHOR	⭐ ⭐ ⭐ ⭐ ⭐

FANTASY

TITLE	RATING
AUTHOR	⭐ ⭐ ⭐ ⭐ ⭐

YOUNG ADULT

TITLE	RATING
AUTHOR	⭐ ⭐ ⭐ ⭐ ⭐

BEACH READ

TITLE	RATING
AUTHOR	⭐ ⭐ ⭐ ⭐ ⭐

SPIRITUAL

TITLE	RATING
AUTHOR	⭐ ⭐ ⭐ ⭐ ⭐

Books Borrowed

TITLE	BORROWED FROM	RETURN DATE

Books Lent Out

TITLE	BORROWER'S NAME	RETURN DATE

Book Review

BOOK #

eBook ○ audiobook ○
hardback ○ paperback ○

_____
TITLE

_____
AUTHOR

STARTED ON	FINISHED ON
/ /	/ /

RATING ☆ ☆ ☆ ☆ ☆

LENGTH _____ pgs.

GENRE _____

RECOMMENDED BY _____

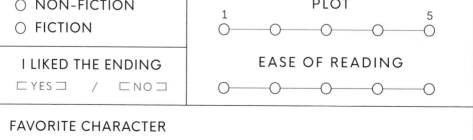

○ NON-FICTION
○ FICTION

I LIKED THE ENDING
⊏ YES ⊐ / ⊏ NO ⊐

PLOT
1   5
○——○——○——○——○

EASE OF READING
○——○——○——○——○

FAVORITE CHARACTER

FAVORITE QUOTES

66

99

REVIEW NOTES

I WOULD ASK THE AUTHOR...

WOULD RECOMMEND?   ⊏ YES ⊐   /   ⊏ NO ⊐

Book Review

BOOK #

eBook ○ audiobook ○
hardback ○ paperback ○

_____
TITLE

_____
AUTHOR

STARTED ON	FINISHED ON
/ /	/ /

RATING ☆ ☆ ☆ ☆ ☆

GENRE _____

RECOMMENDED BY _____

LENGTH
_____
pgs.

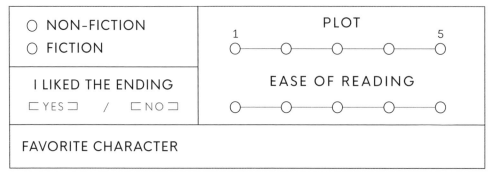

○ NON-FICTION
○ FICTION

I LIKED THE ENDING
⊏ YES ⊐ / ⊏ NO ⊐

PLOT
1 ○——○——○——○——○ 5

EASE OF READING
○——○——○——○——○

FAVORITE CHARACTER

FAVORITE QUOTES

66

_____

_____

_____

_____

_____

_____

_____

99

REVIEW NOTES

_____

_____

_____

_____

_____

_____

_____

_____

_____

_____

_____

_____

_____

I WOULD ASK THE AUTHOR...

_____

_____

WOULD RECOMMEND?　　　⊏ YES ⊐　　/　　⊏ NO ⊐

Book Review

BOOK #

eBook ○   audiobook ○
hardback ○   paperback ○

_____
TITLE

_____
AUTHOR

STARTED ON	FINISHED ON
/ /	/ /

RATING ☆ ☆ ☆ ☆ ☆

LENGTH
____ pgs.

GENRE _____

RECOMMENDED BY _____

○ NON-FICTION ○ FICTION	PLOT 1 ○——○——○——○——○ 5
I LIKED THE ENDING ⊏ YES ⊐ / ⊏ NO ⊐	EASE OF READING ○——○——○——○——○
FAVORITE CHARACTER	

FAVORITE QUOTES

66

_____

_____

_____

_____

_____

_____

_____

99

REVIEW NOTES

_____

_____

_____

_____

_____

_____

_____

_____

_____

_____

_____

I WOULD ASK THE AUTHOR...

_____

_____

WOULD RECOMMEND?   ⊏ YES ⊐   /   ⊏ NO ⊐

Book Review

BOOK #

eBook ○   audiobook ○
hardback ○   paperback ○

_____
TITLE

_____
AUTHOR

STARTED ON	FINISHED ON
/ /	/ /

RATING ☆ ☆ ☆ ☆ ☆

LENGTH

_____ pgs.

GENRE _____

RECOMMENDED BY _____

○ NON-FICTION
○ FICTION

I LIKED THE ENDING
⊏ YES ⊐   /   ⊏ NO ⊐

PLOT
1   5
○———○———○———○———○

EASE OF READING
○———○———○———○———○

FAVORITE CHARACTER

FAVORITE QUOTES

66

_____

_____

_____

_____

_____

_____

_____

_____

99

REVIEW NOTES

_____

_____

_____

_____

_____

_____

_____

_____

_____

_____

_____

_____

_____

I WOULD ASK THE AUTHOR...

_____

_____

WOULD RECOMMEND?   ⊏ YES ⊐   /   ⊏ NO ⊐

Book Review

BOOK #

eBook ○ audiobook ○
hardback ○ paperback ○

_____

TITLE

_____

AUTHOR

STARTED ON	FINISHED ON
/ /	/ /

RATING ☆ ☆ ☆ ☆ ☆

LENGTH

_____ pgs.

GENRE _____

RECOMMENDED BY _____

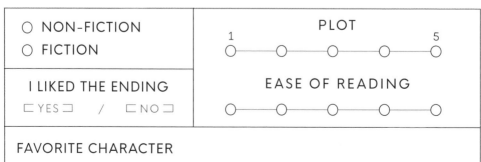

○ NON-FICTION
○ FICTION

PLOT
1   5
○——○——○——○——○

I LIKED THE ENDING
⊏ YES ⊐ / ⊏ NO ⊐

EASE OF READING
○——○——○——○——○

FAVORITE CHARACTER

66

99

I WOULD ASK THE AUTHOR...

WOULD RECOMMEND?   ⊏ YES ⊐   /   ⊏ NO ⊐

Book Review

BOOK #

eBook ○ audiobook ○
hardback ○ paperback ○

_____
TITLE

_____
AUTHOR

STARTED ON	FINISHED ON
/ /	/ /

RATING ☆ ☆ ☆ ☆ ☆

GENRE _____

LENGTH
_____
pgs.

RECOMMENDED BY _____

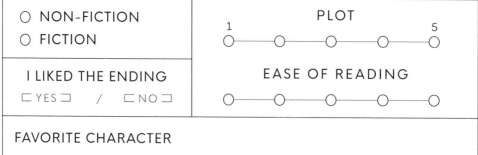

○ NON-FICTION
○ FICTION

PLOT
1   5
○——○——○——○——○

I LIKED THE ENDING
⊏ YES ⊐ / ⊏ NO ⊐

EASE OF READING
○——○——○——○——○

FAVORITE CHARACTER

FAVORITE QUOTES

"

"

REVIEW NOTES

I WOULD ASK THE AUTHOR...

WOULD RECOMMEND?   ⊏ YES ⊐   /   ⊏ NO ⊐

Book Review

BOOK #

eBook ○ audiobook ○
hardback ○ paperback ○

_____

TITLE

_____

AUTHOR

STARTED ON	FINISHED ON
/ /	/ /

RATING ☆ ☆ ☆ ☆ ☆

LENGTH
_____ pgs.

GENRE _____

RECOMMENDED BY _____

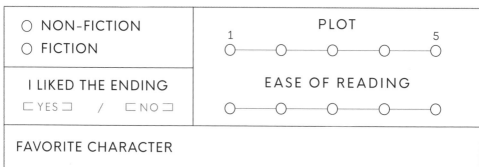

○ NON-FICTION
○ FICTION

PLOT
1 ○——○——○——○——○ 5

I LIKED THE ENDING
⊏ YES ⊐ / ⊏ NO ⊐

EASE OF READING
○——○——○——○——○

FAVORITE CHARACTER

FAVORITE QUOTES

66

_____

_____

_____

_____

_____

_____

_____

99

REVIEW NOTES

_____

_____

_____

_____

_____

_____

_____

_____

_____

_____

_____

_____

_____

I WOULD ASK THE AUTHOR...

_____

_____

WOULD RECOMMEND?   ⊏ YES ⊐   /   ⊏ NO ⊐

Book Review

BOOK #

eBook ○   audiobook ○
hardback ○   paperback ○

_____

TITLE

_____

AUTHOR

STARTED ON	FINISHED ON
/ /	/ /

RATING ☆ ☆ ☆ ☆ ☆

LENGTH
_____ pgs.

GENRE _____

RECOMMENDED BY _____

○ NON-FICTION ○ FICTION	PLOT 1 ──○──○──○──○──○── 5
I LIKED THE ENDING ⊏ YES ⊐ / ⊏ NO ⊐	EASE OF READING ○──○──○──○──○
FAVORITE CHARACTER	

FAVORITE QUOTES

66

_____

_____

_____

_____

_____

_____

_____

99

REVIEW NOTES

_____

_____

_____

_____

_____

_____

_____

_____

_____

_____

_____

I WOULD ASK THE AUTHOR…

_____

_____

WOULD RECOMMEND?   ⊏ YES ⊐   /   ⊏ NO ⊐

Book Review

BOOK #

eBook ○ audiobook ○
hardback ○ paperback ○

_____
TITLE

_____
AUTHOR

| STARTED ON | FINISHED ON |
| / / | / / |

RATING ☆ ☆ ☆ ☆ ☆

LENGTH

_____ pgs.

GENRE _____

RECOMMENDED BY _____

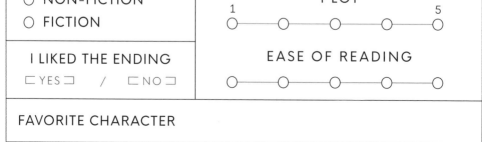

○ NON-FICTION
○ FICTION

PLOT
1   5
○──○──○──○──○

I LIKED THE ENDING
⊏ YES ⊐ / ⊏ NO ⊐

EASE OF READING
○──○──○──○──○

FAVORITE CHARACTER

66

_____

_____

_____

_____

_____

_____

_____

99

_____

_____

_____

_____

_____

_____

_____

_____

_____

_____

_____

_____

I WOULD ASK THE AUTHOR...

_____

_____

WOULD RECOMMEND?   ⊏ YES ⊐   /   ⊏ NO ⊐

BOOK #

eBook ○ audiobook ○
hardback ○ paperback ○

_____

TITLE

_____

AUTHOR

STARTED ON	FINISHED ON
/ /	/ /

LENGTH

_____ pgs.

RATING ☆ ☆ ☆ ☆ ☆

GENRE _____

RECOMMENDED BY _____

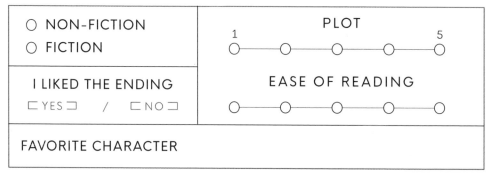

○ NON-FICTION
○ FICTION

PLOT
1 ○—○—○—○—○ 5

I LIKED THE ENDING
⌐YES⌐ / ⌐NO⌐

EASE OF READING
○—○—○—○—○

FAVORITE CHARACTER

FAVORITE QUOTES

66

_____

_____

_____

_____

_____

_____

_____

99

REVIEW NOTES

_____

_____

_____

_____

_____

_____

_____

_____

_____

_____

_____

_____

I WOULD ASK THE AUTHOR...

_____

_____

WOULD RECOMMEND?   ⊏ YES ⊐   /   ⊏ NO ⊐

Book Review

BOOK #

eBook ○   audiobook ○
hardback ○   paperback ○

_____
TITLE

_____
AUTHOR

STARTED ON	FINISHED ON
/ /	/ /

RATING ☆ ☆ ☆ ☆ ☆

GENRE _____

LENGTH

_____ pgs.

RECOMMENDED BY _____

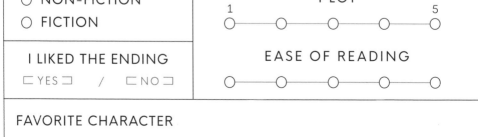

○ NON-FICTION
○ FICTION

PLOT

1   5
○——○——○——○——○

I LIKED THE ENDING

⊏ YES ⊐ / ⊏ NO ⊐

EASE OF READING

○——○——○——○——○

FAVORITE CHARACTER

FAVORITE QUOTES

REVIEW NOTES

I WOULD ASK THE AUTHOR...

WOULD RECOMMEND?   ⊏ YES⊐   /   ⊏ NO⊐

Book Review

BOOK #

eBook○ audiobook○
hardback○ paperback○

_____
TITLE

_____
AUTHOR

STARTED ON	FINISHED ON
/ /	/ /

RATING ☆ ☆ ☆ ☆ ☆

GENRE _____

RECOMMENDED BY _____

LENGTH
_____ pgs.

○ NON-FICTION
○ FICTION

PLOT
1   5
○—○—○—○—○

I LIKED THE ENDING
⊏ YES ⊐ / ⊏ NO ⊐

EASE OF READING
○—○—○—○—○

FAVORITE CHARACTER

FAVORITE QUOTES

REVIEW NOTES

I WOULD ASK THE AUTHOR...

WOULD RECOMMEND?   ⊏ YES⊐   /   ⊏ NO⊐

Book Review

BOOK #

eBook ○   audiobook ○
hardback ○   paperback ○

_____
TITLE

_____
AUTHOR

STARTED ON	FINISHED ON
/ /	/ /

LENGTH
_____ pgs.

RATING ☆ ☆ ☆ ☆ ☆

GENRE _____

RECOMMENDED BY _____

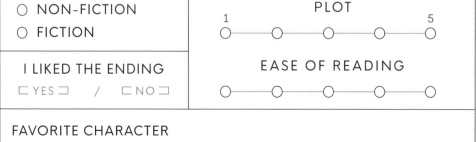

○ NON-FICTION
○ FICTION

I LIKED THE ENDING
⊏ YES ⊐   /   ⊏ NO ⊐

PLOT
1   5
○——○——○——○——○

EASE OF READING
○——○——○——○——○

FAVORITE CHARACTER

FAVORITE QUOTES

66

99

REVIEW NOTES

I WOULD ASK THE AUTHOR...

WOULD RECOMMEND?   ⊏ YES ⊐   /   ⊏ NO ⊐

Book Review

BOOK #

eBook ○   audiobook ○
hardback ○   paperback ○

_____
TITLE

_____
AUTHOR

STARTED ON	FINISHED ON
/ /	/ /

RATING ☆ ☆ ☆ ☆ ☆

LENGTH
_____ pgs.

GENRE _____

RECOMMENDED BY _____

○ NON-FICTION
○ FICTION

PLOT
1　　　　　　　　　　　　5
○——○——○——○——○

I LIKED THE ENDING
⊏ YES ⊐   /   ⊏ NO ⊐

EASE OF READING
○——○——○——○——○

FAVORITE CHARACTER

FAVORITE QUOTES

66

_____
_____
_____
_____
_____
_____
_____

99

REVIEW NOTES

_____
_____
_____
_____
_____
_____
_____
_____
_____
_____
_____
_____
_____

I WOULD ASK THE AUTHOR...

_____
_____

WOULD RECOMMEND?   ⊏ YES⊐   /   ⊏ NO⊐

Book Review

BOOK #

eBook ○   audiobook ○
hardback ○   paperback ○

_____
TITLE

_____
AUTHOR

STARTED ON	FINISHED ON
/ /	/ /

RATING ☆ ☆ ☆ ☆ ☆

LENGTH

_____ pgs.

GENRE _____

RECOMMENDED BY _____

○ NON-FICTION
○ FICTION

PLOT
1 ○——○——○——○——○ 5

I LIKED THE ENDING
⌐ YES ⌐   /   ⌐ NO ⌐

EASE OF READING
○——○——○——○——○

FAVORITE CHARACTER

FAVORITE QUOTES

REVIEW NOTES

I WOULD ASK THE AUTHOR...

WOULD RECOMMEND?   ⊏ YES⊐   /   ⊏ NO⊐

Book Review

BOOK #

eBook ○   audiobook ○
hardback ○   paperback ○

_____
TITLE

_____
AUTHOR

STARTED ON	FINISHED ON
/ /	/ /

RATING ☆ ☆ ☆ ☆ ☆

LENGTH

_____ pgs.

GENRE _____

RECOMMENDED BY _____

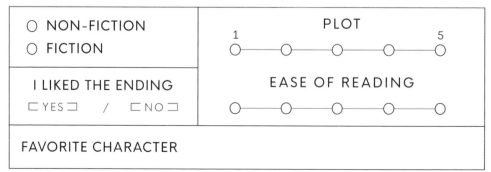

○ NON-FICTION
○ FICTION

I LIKED THE ENDING
⊏ YES ⊐   /   ⊏ NO ⊐

PLOT
1 ○——○——○——○——○ 5

EASE OF READING
○——○——○——○——○

FAVORITE CHARACTER

FAVORITE QUOTES

66

_____

_____

_____

_____

_____

_____

_____

99

REVIEW NOTES

_____

_____

_____

_____

_____

_____

_____

_____

_____

_____

_____

_____

_____

I WOULD ASK THE AUTHOR...

_____

_____

_____

WOULD RECOMMEND?   ⊏ YES ⊐   /   ⊏ NO ⊐

Book Review

BOOK #

eBook ○ audiobook ○
hardback ○ paperback ○

_____

TITLE

_____

AUTHOR

STARTED ON	FINISHED ON
/ /	/ /

RATING ☆ ☆ ☆ ☆ ☆

LENGTH

_____ pgs.

GENRE _____

RECOMMENDED BY _____

○ NON-FICTION
○ FICTION

PLOT

1 ⦿——○——○——○——5 ○

I LIKED THE ENDING

⊏ YES ⊐ / ⊏ NO ⊐

EASE OF READING

○——○——○——○——○

FAVORITE CHARACTER

FAVORITE QUOTES

66

_____

_____

_____

_____

_____

_____

_____

99

REVIEW NOTES

_____

_____

_____

_____

_____

_____

_____

_____

_____

_____

_____

_____

I WOULD ASK THE AUTHOR...

_____

_____

WOULD RECOMMEND?   ⊏ YES ⊐   /   ⊏ NO ⊐

BOOK #

eBook ○ audiobook ○
hardback ○ paperback ○

_____

TITLE

_____

AUTHOR

STARTED ON	FINISHED ON
/ /	/ /

RATING ☆ ☆ ☆ ☆ ☆

LENGTH

_____ pgs.

GENRE _____

RECOMMENDED BY _____

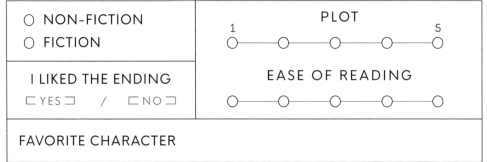

○ NON-FICTION
○ FICTION

PLOT
1 ○——○——○——○——○ 5

I LIKED THE ENDING
⊏ YES ⊐ / ⊏ NO ⊐

EASE OF READING
○——○——○——○——○

FAVORITE CHARACTER

FAVORITE QUOTES

> 66
>
> _____
>
> _____
>
> _____
>
> _____
>
> _____
>
> _____
>
> _____ 99

REVIEW NOTES

_____

_____

_____

_____

_____

_____

_____

_____

_____

_____

_____

_____

_____

I WOULD ASK THE AUTHOR...

_____

_____

WOULD RECOMMEND?   ⊏ YES⊐   /   ⊏ NO⊐

Book Review

BOOK #

eBook ○ audiobook ○
hardback ○ paperback ○

_____
TITLE

_____
AUTHOR

STARTED ON	FINISHED ON
/ /	/ /

LENGTH

RATING ☆ ☆ ☆ ☆ ☆

_____ pgs.

GENRE _____

RECOMMENDED BY _____

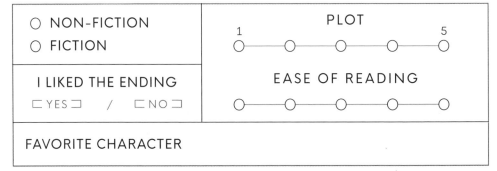

○ NON-FICTION
○ FICTION

PLOT
1   5
○—○—○—○—○

I LIKED THE ENDING
⌐YES⌐ / ⌐NO⌐

EASE OF READING
○—○—○—○—○

FAVORITE CHARACTER

FAVORITE QUOTES

" "

REVIEW NOTES

I WOULD ASK THE AUTHOR...

WOULD RECOMMEND?   ⊏ YES ⊐   /   ⊏ NO ⊐

Book Review

BOOK #

eBook ○ audiobook ○
hardback ○ paperback ○

_____
TITLE

_____
AUTHOR

STARTED ON	FINISHED ON
/ /	/ /

RATING ☆ ☆ ☆ ☆ ☆

LENGTH
_____ pgs.

GENRE _____

RECOMMENDED BY _____

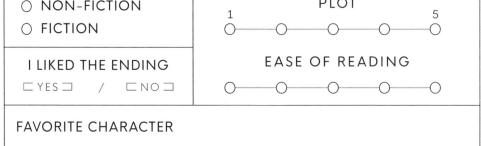

○ NON-FICTION
○ FICTION

I LIKED THE ENDING
⊏ YES ⊐ / ⊏ NO ⊐

PLOT
1 ○——○——○——○——○ 5

EASE OF READING
○——○——○——○——○

FAVORITE CHARACTER

FAVORITE QUOTES

"

"

REVIEW NOTES

I WOULD ASK THE AUTHOR...

WOULD RECOMMEND?   ⊏ YES ⊐   /   ⊏ NO ⊐

Book Review

BOOK #

eBook ○ audiobook ○
hardback ○ paperback ○

_____
TITLE

_____
AUTHOR

STARTED ON	FINISHED ON
/ /	/ /

LENGTH

_____
pgs.

RATING ☆ ☆ ☆ ☆ ☆

GENRE _____

RECOMMENDED BY _____

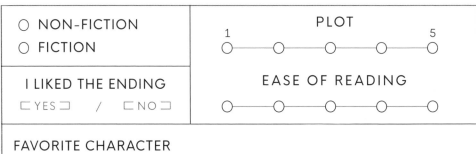

○ NON-FICTION
○ FICTION

PLOT

1   5
○——○——○——○——○

I LIKED THE ENDING

▢ YES ▢   /   ▢ NO ▢

EASE OF READING

○——○——○——○——○

FAVORITE CHARACTER

FAVORITE QUOTES

66

_____

_____

_____

_____

_____

_____

_____

99

REVIEW NOTES

_____

_____

_____

_____

_____

_____

_____

_____

_____

_____

_____

_____

_____

I WOULD ASK THE AUTHOR...

_____

_____

WOULD RECOMMEND?   ⊏ YES⊐   /   ⊏ NO⊐

Book Review

BOOK

eBook ○   audiobook ○
hardback ○   paperback ○

_____

TITLE

_____

AUTHOR

STARTED ON	FINISHED ON
/ /	/ /

RATING ☆ ☆ ☆ ☆ ☆

LENGTH

_____ pgs.

GENRE _____

RECOMMENDED BY _____

○ NON-FICTION
○ FICTION

I LIKED THE ENDING
⊏ YES ⊐ / ⊏ NO ⊐

PLOT
1 ○——○——○——○——○ 5

EASE OF READING
○——○——○——○——○

FAVORITE CHARACTER

FAVORITE QUOTES

66

_____

_____

_____

_____

_____

_____

_____

99

REVIEW NOTES

_____

_____

_____

_____

_____

_____

_____

_____

_____

_____

_____

_____

I WOULD ASK THE AUTHOR...

_____

_____

WOULD RECOMMEND?   ☐ YES ☐   /   ☐ NO ☐

Book Review

BOOK #

eBook ○   audiobook ○
hardback ○   paperback ○

_____
TITLE

_____
AUTHOR

STARTED ON	FINISHED ON
/ /	/ /

RATING ☆ ☆ ☆ ☆ ☆

LENGTH

_____ pgs.

GENRE _____

RECOMMENDED BY _____

○ NON-FICTION
○ FICTION

PLOT
1   5
○——○——○——○——○

I LIKED THE ENDING
⊏ YES ⊐   /   ⊏ NO ⊐

EASE OF READING
○——○——○——○——○

FAVORITE CHARACTER

FAVORITE QUOTES

66

99

REVIEW NOTES

I WOULD ASK THE AUTHOR...

WOULD RECOMMEND?   ⊏ YES ⊐   /   ⊏ NO ⊐

BOOK #

eBook ○   audiobook ○
hardback ○   paperback ○

_____
TITLE

_____
AUTHOR

STARTED ON	FINISHED ON
/ /	/ /

LENGTH
_____ pgs.

RATING ☆ ☆ ☆ ☆ ☆

GENRE _____

RECOMMENDED BY _____

○ NON-FICTION
○ FICTION

PLOT
1   5
○——○——○——○——○

I LIKED THE ENDING
⊏ YES ⊐   /   ⊏ NO ⊐

EASE OF READING
○——○——○——○——○

FAVORITE CHARACTER

FAVORITE QUOTES

66

"

REVIEW NOTES

I WOULD ASK THE AUTHOR...

WOULD RECOMMEND?   ⊏ YES ⊐   /   ⊏ NO ⊐

Book Review

BOOK #

eBook ○ audiobook ○
hardback ○ paperback ○

_____

TITLE

_____

AUTHOR

STARTED ON	FINISHED ON
/ /	/ /

LENGTH

_____ pgs.

RATING ☆ ☆ ☆ ☆ ☆

GENRE _____

RECOMMENDED BY _____

○ NON-FICTION
○ FICTION

PLOT

1   5
○——○——○——○——○

I LIKED THE ENDING

⊏ YES ⊐ / ⊏ NO ⊐

EASE OF READING

○——○——○——○——○

FAVORITE CHARACTER

FAVORITE QUOTES

❝

REVIEW NOTES

I WOULD ASK THE AUTHOR...

WOULD RECOMMEND? ⊏ YES ⊐ / ⊏ NO ⊐

Book Review

BOOK #

eBook ○ audiobook ○
hardback ○ paperback ○

_____
TITLE

_____
AUTHOR

STARTED ON	FINISHED ON
/ /	/ /

RATING ☆ ☆ ☆ ☆ ☆

LENGTH

_____ pgs.

GENRE _____

RECOMMENDED BY _____

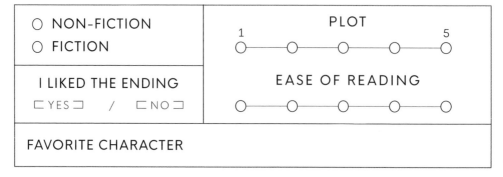

○ NON-FICTION
○ FICTION

PLOT
1 ○——○——○——○——○ 5

I LIKED THE ENDING
⊏ YES ⊐ / ⊏ NO ⊐

EASE OF READING
○——○——○——○——○

FAVORITE CHARACTER

FAVORITE QUOTES

"

_____
_____
_____
_____
_____
_____
_____
_____

"

REVIEW NOTES

_____
_____
_____
_____
_____
_____
_____
_____
_____
_____
_____
_____
_____
_____

I WOULD ASK THE AUTHOR...

_____
_____

WOULD RECOMMEND?   ⊏ YES ⊐   /   ⊏ NO ⊐

Book Review

BOOK #

eBook ○   audiobook ○
hardback ○   paperback ○

_____
TITLE

_____
AUTHOR

STARTED ON	FINISHED ON
/ /	/ /

RATING ☆ ☆ ☆ ☆ ☆

LENGTH
_____ pgs.

GENRE _____

RECOMMENDED BY _____

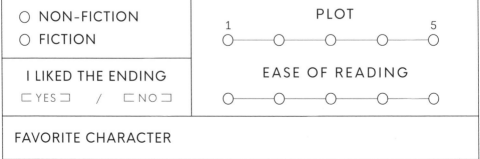

○ NON-FICTION
○ FICTION

PLOT
1   5
○——○——○——○——○

I LIKED THE ENDING
⊏ YES ⊐ / ⊏ NO ⊐

EASE OF READING
○——○——○——○——○

FAVORITE CHARACTER

FAVORITE QUOTES

66

_____

_____

_____

_____

_____

_____

_____

99

REVIEW NOTES

_____

_____

_____

_____

_____

_____

_____

_____

_____

_____

_____

_____

I WOULD ASK THE AUTHOR...

_____

_____

WOULD RECOMMEND?   ⊏ YES ⊐   /   ⊏ NO ⊐

Book Review

BOOK #

eBook○ audiobook○
hardback○ paperback○

_____
TITLE

_____
AUTHOR

| STARTED ON | FINISHED ON |
| / / | / / |

RATING ☆ ☆ ☆ ☆ ☆

LENGTH
_____ pgs.

GENRE _____

RECOMMENDED BY _____

○ NON-FICTION
○ FICTION

PLOT
1　　　　　　　　　　　5
○——○——○——○——○

I LIKED THE ENDING
⊏ YES ⊐ / ⊏ NO ⊐

EASE OF READING
○——○——○——○——○

FAVORITE CHARACTER

FAVORITE QUOTES

"

"

REVIEW NOTES

I WOULD ASK THE AUTHOR...

WOULD RECOMMEND?   ⊏ YES ⊐   /   ⊏ NO ⊐

Book Review

BOOK #

eBook ○   audiobook ○
hardback ○   paperback ○

_____
TITLE

_____
AUTHOR

| STARTED ON | FINISHED ON |
| / / | / / |

RATING ☆ ☆ ☆ ☆ ☆

LENGTH
_____ pgs.

GENRE _____

RECOMMENDED BY _____

○ NON-FICTION
○ FICTION

PLOT
1   5
○—○—○—○—○

I LIKED THE ENDING
YES / NO

EASE OF READING
○—○—○—○—○

FAVORITE CHARACTER

66

_____

_____

_____

_____

_____

_____

_____

_____

99

_____

_____

_____

_____

_____

_____

_____

_____

_____

_____

_____

_____

_____

_____

I WOULD ASK THE AUTHOR...

_____

_____

WOULD RECOMMEND?   ⊏ YES ⊐   /   ⊏ NO ⊐

Book Review

BOOK #

eBook ○   audiobook ○
hardback ○   paperback ○

_____
TITLE

_____
AUTHOR

STARTED ON	FINISHED ON
/ /	/ /

RATING ☆ ☆ ☆ ☆ ☆

LENGTH
_____ pgs.

GENRE _____

RECOMMENDED BY _____

○ NON-FICTION
○ FICTION

PLOT
1   5
○——○——○——○——○

I LIKED THE ENDING
⊏ YES ⊐   /   ⊏ NO ⊐

EASE OF READING
○——○——○——○——○

FAVORITE CHARACTER

FAVORITE QUOTES

"

"

REVIEW NOTES

I WOULD ASK THE AUTHOR...

WOULD RECOMMEND?   ⊏ YES ⊐   /   ⊏ NO ⊐

Book Review

BOOK #

eBook ○ audiobook ○
hardback ○ paperback ○

_____

TITLE

_____

AUTHOR

STARTED ON	FINISHED ON
/ /	/ /

RATING ☆ ☆ ☆ ☆ ☆

LENGTH

_____ pgs.

GENRE _____

RECOMMENDED BY _____

○ NON-FICTION
○ FICTION

PLOT

1   5
○——○——○——○——○

I LIKED THE ENDING

⊏ YES ⊐ / ⊏ NO ⊐

EASE OF READING

○——○——○——○——○

FAVORITE CHARACTER

FAVORITE QUOTES

66

_____

_____

_____

_____

_____

_____

_____

99

REVIEW NOTES

_____

_____

_____

_____

_____

_____

_____

_____

_____

_____

_____

I WOULD ASK THE AUTHOR...

_____

_____

WOULD RECOMMEND?   ⊏ YES⊐   /   ⊏ NO⊐

Book Review

BOOK #

eBook ○ audiobook ○
hardback ○ paperback ○

_____
TITLE

_____
AUTHOR

STARTED ON	FINISHED ON
/ /	/ /

LENGTH

RATING ☆ ☆ ☆ ☆ ☆

_____ pgs.

GENRE _____

RECOMMENDED BY _____

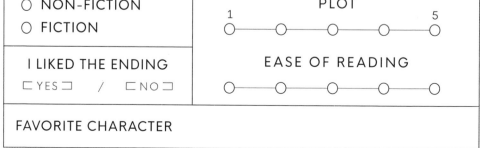

○ NON-FICTION
○ FICTION

PLOT
1   ○——○——○——○——○   5

I LIKED THE ENDING
⊏ YES ⊐ / ⊏ NO ⊐

EASE OF READING
○——○——○——○——○

FAVORITE CHARACTER

66

_____

_____

_____

_____

_____

_____

_____

_____ 99

REVIEW NOTES

_____

_____

_____

_____

_____

_____

_____

_____

_____

_____

_____

_____

_____

I WOULD ASK THE AUTHOR...

_____

_____

_____

| WOULD RECOMMEND? | ☐ YES ☐ | / | ☐ NO ☐ |

Book Review

BOOK #

eBook ○ audiobook ○
hardback ○ paperback ○

_____

TITLE

_____

AUTHOR

STARTED ON	FINISHED ON
/ /	/ /

RATING ☆ ☆ ☆ ☆ ☆

LENGTH _____ pgs.

GENRE _____

RECOMMENDED BY _____

○ NON-FICTION
○ FICTION

PLOT
1 ○—○—○—○—○ 5

I LIKED THE ENDING
⊏ YES ⊐ / ⊏ NO ⊐

EASE OF READING
○—○—○—○—○

FAVORITE CHARACTER

FAVORITE QUOTES

66

_____
_____
_____
_____
_____
_____
_____

99

REVIEW NOTES

_____
_____
_____
_____
_____
_____
_____
_____
_____
_____
_____
_____
_____

I WOULD ASK THE AUTHOR...

_____
_____
_____

WOULD RECOMMEND?   ⊏ YES ⊐   /   ⊏ NO ⊐

BOOK #

eBook ○   audiobook ○
hardback ○   paperback ○

_____

TITLE

_____

AUTHOR

STARTED ON	FINISHED ON
/ /	/ /

RATING ☆ ☆ ☆ ☆ ☆

LENGTH
_____ pgs.

GENRE _____

RECOMMENDED BY _____

○ NON-FICTION
○ FICTION

I LIKED THE ENDING
⊏ YES ⊐ / ⊏ NO ⊐

PLOT
1   5
○——○——○——○——○

EASE OF READING
○——○——○——○——○

FAVORITE CHARACTER

66

99

I WOULD ASK THE AUTHOR...

WOULD RECOMMEND?   ⊏ YES ⊐   /   ⊏ NO ⊐

BOOK #

eBook○ audiobook○
hardback○ paperback○

_____
TITLE

_____
AUTHOR

STARTED ON	FINISHED ON
/ /	/ /

RATING ☆ ☆ ☆ ☆ ☆

LENGTH
_____ pgs.

GENRE _____

RECOMMENDED BY _____

○ NON-FICTION
○ FICTION

PLOT
1   5
○──○──○──○──○

I LIKED THE ENDING
⊏ YES ⊐ / ⊏ NO ⊐

EASE OF READING
○──○──○──○──○

FAVORITE CHARACTER

FAVORITE QUOTES

66

99

REVIEW NOTES

I WOULD ASK THE AUTHOR...

WOULD RECOMMEND?   ⊏ YES ⊐   /   ⊏ NO ⊐

Book Review

BOOK #

eBook ○ audiobook ○
hardback ○ paperback ○

_____

TITLE

_____

AUTHOR

STARTED ON	FINISHED ON
/ /	/ /

RATING ☆ ☆ ☆ ☆ ☆

GENRE _____

RECOMMENDED BY _____

LENGTH
_____ pgs.

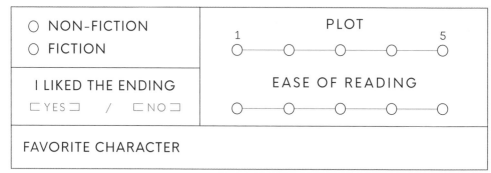

○ NON-FICTION
○ FICTION

PLOT
1 ○——○——○——○ 5

I LIKED THE ENDING
⊏ YES ⊐ / ⊏ NO ⊐

EASE OF READING
○——○——○——○——○

FAVORITE CHARACTER

FAVORITE QUOTES

"

"

REVIEW NOTES

I WOULD ASK THE AUTHOR...

WOULD RECOMMEND?   ⊏ YES ⊐   /   ⊏ NO ⊐

Book Review

BOOK

eBook ○   audiobook ○
hardback ○   paperback ○

_____
TITLE

_____
AUTHOR

STARTED ON	FINISHED ON
/ /	/ /

RATING ☆ ☆ ☆ ☆ ☆

GENRE _____

RECOMMENDED BY _____

LENGTH
_____ pgs.

○ NON-FICTION ○ FICTION	PLOT 1 ○──○──○──○──○ 5
I LIKED THE ENDING ⊏ YES ⊐ / ⊏ NO ⊐	EASE OF READING ○──○──○──○──○
FAVORITE CHARACTER	

FAVORITE QUOTES

"

"

REVIEW NOTES

I WOULD ASK THE AUTHOR...

WOULD RECOMMEND?   ⊏ YES ⊐   /   ⊏ NO ⊐

Book Review

BOOK #

eBook ○ audiobook ○
hardback ○ paperback ○

_____

TITLE

_____

AUTHOR

STARTED ON	FINISHED ON
/ /	/ /

LENGTH

_____ pgs.

RATING ☆ ☆ ☆ ☆ ☆

GENRE _____

RECOMMENDED BY _____

○ NON-FICTION
○ FICTION

PLOT
1 ○──○──○──○──○ 5

I LIKED THE ENDING
⊏ YES ⊐ / ⊏ NO ⊐

EASE OF READING
○──○──○──○──○

FAVORITE CHARACTER

FAVORITE QUOTES

66

_____

_____

_____

_____

_____

_____

_____

99

REVIEW NOTES

_____

_____

_____

_____

_____

_____

_____

_____

_____

_____

_____

_____

_____

I WOULD ASK THE AUTHOR...

_____

_____

WOULD RECOMMEND?   ⊏ YES ⊐   /   ⊏ NO ⊐

Book Review

BOOK #

eBook ○ audiobook ○
hardback ○ paperback ○

_____
TITLE

_____
AUTHOR

STARTED ON	FINISHED ON
/ /	/ /

RATING ☆ ☆ ☆ ☆ ☆

LENGTH

_____ pgs.

GENRE _____

RECOMMENDED BY _____

○ NON-FICTION
○ FICTION

PLOT

1 ○——○——○——○——○ 5

I LIKED THE ENDING
⊏ YES ⊐ / ⊏ NO ⊐

EASE OF READING

○——○——○——○——○

FAVORITE CHARACTER

FAVORITE QUOTES

66

_____

_____

_____

_____

_____

_____

_____

99

REVIEW NOTES

_____

_____

_____

_____

_____

_____

_____

_____

_____

_____

_____

_____

I WOULD ASK THE AUTHOR...

_____

_____

WOULD RECOMMEND?   ⊏ YES⊐   /   ⊏ NO⊐

Book Review

BOOK #

eBook○ audiobook○
hardback○ paperback○

_____
TITLE

_____
AUTHOR

STARTED ON	FINISHED ON
/ /	/ /

RATING ☆ ☆ ☆ ☆ ☆

GENRE _____

RECOMMENDED BY _____

LENGTH

_____ pgs.

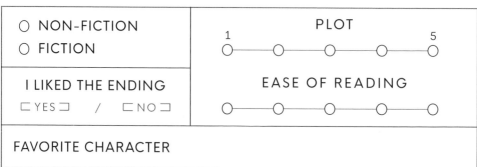

○ NON-FICTION
○ FICTION

PLOT
1 ○——○——○——○——○ 5

I LIKED THE ENDING
⊏ YES ⊐ / ⊏ NO ⊐

EASE OF READING
○——○——○——○——○

FAVORITE CHARACTER

FAVORITE QUOTES

66

99

REVIEW NOTES

I WOULD ASK THE AUTHOR...

WOULD RECOMMEND?   ⊏ YES ⊐   /   ⊏ NO ⊐

BOOK #

eBook ○   audiobook ○
hardback ○   paperback ○

_____

TITLE

_____

AUTHOR

STARTED ON	FINISHED ON
/ /	/ /

RATING ☆ ☆ ☆ ☆ ☆

LENGTH
_____ pgs.

GENRE _____

RECOMMENDED BY _____

○ NON-FICTION
○ FICTION

PLOT
1 ○——○——○——○——○ 5

I LIKED THE ENDING
⊏ YES ⊐   /   ⊏ NO ⊐

EASE OF READING
○——○——○——○——○

FAVORITE CHARACTER

FAVORITE QUOTES

66

99

REVIEW NOTES

I WOULD ASK THE AUTHOR...

WOULD RECOMMEND?   ⊏ YES ⊐   /   ⊏ NO ⊐

Book Review

BOOK #

eBook ○ audiobook ○
hardback ○ paperback ○

_____

TITLE

_____

AUTHOR

STARTED ON	FINISHED ON
/ /	/ /

RATING ☆ ☆ ☆ ☆ ☆

GENRE _____

RECOMMENDED BY _____

LENGTH
_____ pgs.

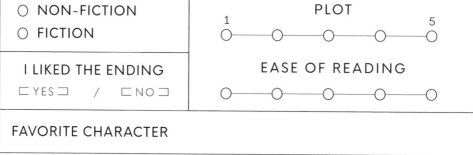

○ NON-FICTION
○ FICTION

I LIKED THE ENDING
▢ YES ▢ / ▢ NO ▢

PLOT
1   5
○——○——○——○——○

EASE OF READING
○———○———○———○———○

FAVORITE CHARACTER

66

_____

_____

_____

_____

_____

_____

_____

99

REVIEW NOTES

_____

_____

_____

_____

_____

_____

_____

_____

_____

_____

_____

_____

I WOULD ASK THE AUTHOR...

_____

_____

WOULD RECOMMEND?　　⊏ YES ⊐　　/　　⊏ NO ⊐

Book Review

BOOK

eBook ○ audiobook ○
hardback ○ paperback ○

_____
TITLE

_____
AUTHOR

STARTED ON	FINISHED ON
/ /	/ /

RATING ☆ ☆ ☆ ☆ ☆

LENGTH
_____ pgs.

GENRE _____

RECOMMENDED BY _____

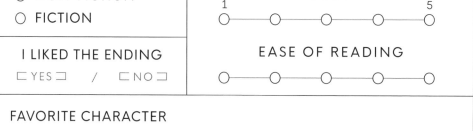

○ NON-FICTION ○ FICTION	**PLOT** 1 ○—○—○—○—○ 5
I LIKED THE ENDING ⊏ YES ⊐ / ⊏ NO ⊐	**EASE OF READING** ○—○—○—○—○

FAVORITE CHARACTER

FAVORITE QUOTES

66

_____
_____
_____
_____
_____
_____
_____
_____

99

REVIEW NOTES

_____
_____
_____
_____
_____
_____
_____
_____
_____
_____
_____
_____

I WOULD ASK THE AUTHOR...

_____
_____

WOULD RECOMMEND?   ⊏ YES ⊐   /   ⊏ NO ⊐

Book Review

BOOK #

eBook○   audiobook○
hardback○   paperback○

_____
TITLE

_____
AUTHOR

| STARTED ON | FINISHED ON |
| / / | / / |

LENGTH

RATING ☆ ☆ ☆ ☆ ☆

_____ pgs.

GENRE _____

RECOMMENDED BY _____

○ NON-FICTION ○ FICTION	PLOT 1 5 ○──○──○──○──○
I LIKED THE ENDING ⊏ YES ⊐ / ⊏ NO ⊐	EASE OF READING ○──○──○──○──○
FAVORITE CHARACTER	

FAVORITE QUOTES

66

_____

_____

_____

_____

_____

_____

_____

99

REVIEW NOTES

_____

_____

_____

_____

_____

_____

_____

_____

_____

_____

_____

_____

I WOULD ASK THE AUTHOR...

_____

_____

WOULD RECOMMEND?   ⊏ YES ⊐   /   ⊏ NO ⊐

Book Review

BOOK #

eBook ○ audiobook ○
hardback ○ paperback ○

_____
TITLE

_____
AUTHOR

STARTED ON	FINISHED ON
/ /	/ /

RATING ☆ ☆ ☆ ☆ ☆

LENGTH
_____ pgs.

GENRE _____

RECOMMENDED BY _____

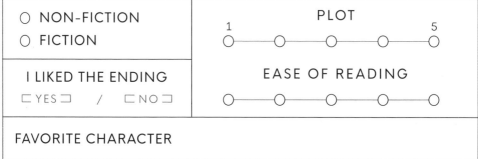

○ NON-FICTION
○ FICTION

I LIKED THE ENDING
⊏ YES ⊐ / ⊏ NO ⊐

PLOT
1 ─○───○───○───○───○─ 5

EASE OF READING
○───○───○───○───○

FAVORITE CHARACTER

FAVORITE QUOTES

"

"

REVIEW NOTES

I WOULD ASK THE AUTHOR...

WOULD RECOMMEND?　　　☐ YES☐　　/　　☐ NO☐

BOOK #

eBook ○   audiobook ○
hardback ○   paperback ○

_____

TITLE

_____

AUTHOR

STARTED ON	FINISHED ON
/ /	/ /

RATING ☆ ☆ ☆ ☆ ☆

LENGTH

_____ pgs.

GENRE _____

RECOMMENDED BY _____

○ NON-FICTION
○ FICTION

PLOT

1 ○——○——○——○——○ 5

I LIKED THE ENDING

⊏ YES ⊐   /   ⊏ NO ⊐

EASE OF READING

○——○——○——○——○

FAVORITE CHARACTER

FAVORITE QUOTES

❝

❞

REVIEW NOTES

I WOULD ASK THE AUTHOR...

WOULD RECOMMEND?   ⊏ YES ⊐   /   ⊏ NO ⊐

Book Review

BOOK #

eBook○ audiobook○
hardback○ paperback○

_____

TITLE

_____

AUTHOR

STARTED ON	FINISHED ON
/ /	/ /

RATING ☆ ☆ ☆ ☆ ☆

LENGTH

_____ pgs.

GENRE _____

RECOMMENDED BY _____

○ NON-FICTION	PLOT
○ FICTION	1 5
	○─○─○─○─○
I LIKED THE ENDING	EASE OF READING
⌐YES⌐ / ⌐NO⌐	○─○─○─○─○

FAVORITE CHARACTER

FAVORITE QUOTES

"

"

REVIEW NOTES

I WOULD ASK THE AUTHOR...

WOULD RECOMMEND?   ⊏ YES ⊐   /   ⊏ NO ⊐

Book Review

BOOK #

eBook ○   audiobook ○
hardback ○   paperback ○

_____

TITLE

_____

AUTHOR

STARTED ON	FINISHED ON
/ /	/ /

RATING ☆ ☆ ☆ ☆ ☆

L E N G T H

_____ pgs.

GENRE _____

RECOMMENDED BY _____

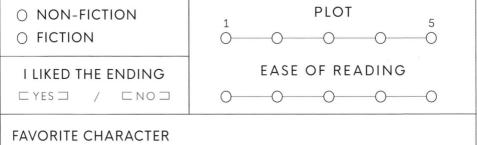

○ NON-FICTION
○ FICTION

PLOT

1   ○——○——○——○——○   5

I LIKED THE ENDING

⊏ YES ⊐   /   ⊏ NO ⊐

EASE OF READING

○——○——○——○——○

FAVORITE CHARACTER

FAVORITE QUOTES

66

"

REVIEW NOTES

I WOULD ASK THE AUTHOR...

WOULD RECOMMEND?   ⊏ YES ⊐   /   ⊏ NO ⊐

Book Review

BOOK #

eBook ○   audiobook ○
hardback ○   paperback ○

_____
TITLE

_____
AUTHOR

STARTED ON	FINISHED ON
/ /	/ /

LENGTH

RATING ☆ ☆ ☆ ☆ ☆

_____ pgs.

GENRE _____

RECOMMENDED BY _____

○ NON-FICTION
○ FICTION

PLOT

1 ○———○———○———○———○ 5

I LIKED THE ENDING

⊏ YES ⊐ / ⊏ NO ⊐

EASE OF READING

○———○———○———○———○

FAVORITE CHARACTER

FAVORITE QUOTES

66

" "

REVIEW NOTES

I WOULD ASK THE AUTHOR...

WOULD RECOMMEND?　　　⊏ YES⊐　　/　　⊏ NO⊐

Book Review

BOOK #

eBook ○   audiobook ○
hardback ○   paperback ○

_____
TITLE

_____
AUTHOR

STARTED ON	FINISHED ON
/ /	/ /

LENGTH

_____ pgs.

RATING ☆ ☆ ☆ ☆ ☆

GENRE _____

RECOMMENDED BY _____

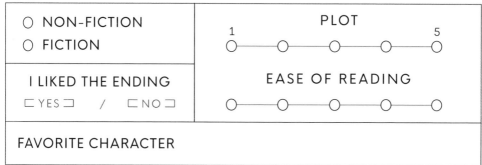

○ NON-FICTION
○ FICTION

PLOT
1 ○—○—○—○—○ 5

I LIKED THE ENDING
⊏ YES ⊐ / ⊏ NO ⊐

EASE OF READING
○—○—○—○—○

FAVORITE CHARACTER

FAVORITE QUOTES

66

99

REVIEW NOTES

I WOULD ASK THE AUTHOR...

| WOULD RECOMMEND? | YES / NO |

Book Review

BOOK #

eBook ○ audiobook ○
hardback ○ paperback ○

_____

TITLE

_____

AUTHOR

STARTED ON	FINISHED ON
/ /	/ /

LENGTH

_____ pgs.

RATING ☆ ☆ ☆ ☆ ☆

GENRE _____

RECOMMENDED BY _____

○ NON-FICTION
○ FICTION

PLOT

1 ○——○——○——○——○ 5

I LIKED THE ENDING

⊏ YES ⊐ / ⊏ NO ⊐

EASE OF READING

○——○——○——○——○

FAVORITE CHARACTER

FAVORITE QUOTES

66

99

REVIEW NOTES

I WOULD ASK THE AUTHOR...

WOULD RECOMMEND?   ⊏ YES ⊐   /   ⊏ NO ⊐

Book Review

BOOK

eBook ○ audiobook ○
hardback ○ paperback ○

_____

TITLE

_____

AUTHOR

STARTED ON	FINISHED ON
/ /	/ /

RATING ☆ ☆ ☆ ☆ ☆

LENGTH

_____ pgs.

GENRE _____

RECOMMENDED BY _____

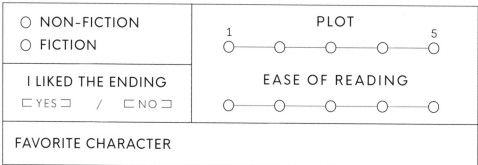

○ NON-FICTION
○ FICTION

PLOT
1   5
○——○——○——○——○

I LIKED THE ENDING
⊏ YES ⊐ / ⊏ NO ⊐

EASE OF READING
○——○——○——○——○

FAVORITE CHARACTER

FAVORITE QUOTES

"

"

REVIEW NOTES

I WOULD ASK THE AUTHOR...

WOULD RECOMMEND?   ⊏ YES ⊐   /   ⊏ NO ⊐